Getting To Know...

Nature's Children

CHIPMUNKS

Merebeth Switzer

Grolier Limited

TORONTO

PUBLISHER	Joseph R. DeVarennes
PUBLICATION DIRECTOR	Kenneth H. Pearson
MANAGING EDITOR	Valerie Wyatt
SERIES ADVISOR	Merebeth Switzer
SERIES CONSULTANT	Michael Singleton
CONSULTANTS	Ross James
	Kay McKeever
	Dr. Audrey N. Tomera
ADVISORS	Roger Aubin
	Robert Furlonger
	Gaston Lavoie
EDITORIAL SUPERVISOR	Jocelyn Smyth
PRODUCTION MANAGER	Ernest Homewood
PRODUCTION ASSISTANTS	Penelope Moir
	Brock Piper
EDITORS	Katherine Farris Anne Minguet-Patocka
	Sandra Gulland Sarah Reid
	Cristel Kleitsch Cathy Ripley
	Elizabeth MacLeod Eleanor Tourtel
	Pamela Martin Karin Velcheff
PHOTO EDITORS	Bill Ivy
	Don Markle
DESIGN	Annette Tatchell
CARTOGRAPHER	Jane Davie
PUBLICATION ADMINISTRATION	Kathy Kishimoto
	Monique Lemonnier
ARTISTS	Marianne Collins Greg Ruhl
	Pat Ivy Mary Theberge

This series is approved and recommended
by the Federation of Ontario Naturalists.

Canadian Cataloguing in Publication Data

Switzer, Merebeth.
  Chipmunks

(Getting to know—nature's children)
Includes index.
ISBN 0-7172-1893-7

1. Chipmunks—Juvenile literature. I. Title
II. Series.

QL737.R68S87 1984   j599.32′32   C84-099389-7

Have you ever wondered . . .

Chipmunks are one of nature's most delightful animals. On summer days, we enjoy seeing them scamper past, their striped cheeks bulging with seeds. With a bit of luck we can sometimes even coax one to come and take a peanut from our hand.

But, friendly as they seem, chipmunks are secretive little animals. It is not likely that you will stumble across their home or that you will see a baby chipmunk.

Sometimes chipmunks seem to be everywhere, but at other times there is not a chipmunk in sight. What happens? Let's look closer and find out.

The tiny chipmunk is a timid creature, but patience—and an appetizing offering—can often overcome its fears.

Where They Live

Most chipmunks live in forests and woods, but some are found at the edge of deserts and high up in the mountains. These places are very different from one another, but they have one important feature in common. In all of them, chipmunks can find hiding places and the low bushes and plants they need for food.

Chipmunks are ground animals, and all of them spend some part of their life in underground homes called burrows. So it is also very important that they live in a place where the soil is dry and easy to dig. This means that you will rarely find chipmunks in swampy areas or in places with heavy clay soil.

Usually chipmunks do not live in towns and cities. If you do meet a chipmunk in or near the city, it will probably be living in an abandoned barn or house on the outskirts of town.

Chipmunks are found across much of North America. Notice, however, that there are none on the tundra, on the Great Plains or in the hot, swampy regions of the South.

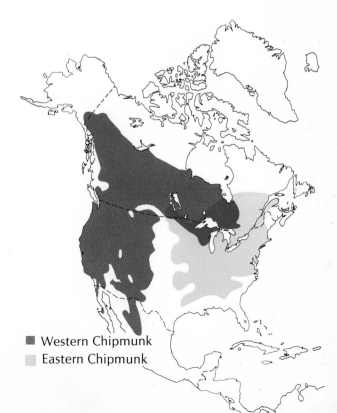

■ Western Chipmunk
■ Eastern Chipmunk

Chipmunks Up Close

We all know the chipmunk with its light brown fur, light underbelly and striped back. If you count the stripes you will find that there are five dark brown stripes separated by four white or beige stripes.

In western regions you might mistake a close relative, the ground squirrel, for the chipmunk. But look closely—there is one easy-to-spot difference. Chipmunks have stripes on their faces, around their eyes, as well as down their backs. Many ground squirrels have plain faces with stripes only on their backs. And if you are close enough to count, you will find that there are different numbers of stripes.

There are many varieties of chipmunk in North America. This means that chipmunks may look quite different depending on where they live.

Chipmunk footprints

Unlike squirrels, chipmunks have stripes on their cheeks as well as on their backs.

The Eastern Chipmunk is the largest and has the shortest tail for its size. The smaller western chipmunks—there are 16 different kinds—are almost all lighter in color. They have longer tails for their size, up to one-half their total length. Western chipmunks spend more time in trees than their eastern cousins, and their long tail probably helps them to balance more easily.

Eastern Chipmunk Length 26 cm (10 in) Weight 100 g (3.5 oz)

Keeping Clean

Just like you, the chipmunk has to keep itself clean. And just like you, it does this by taking a bath. There is one difference, however. The chipmunk takes its bath in dust.

That's right, in dust. The dust helps to clean dirt and extra oil from the chipmunk's fur. It also helps to remove fleas and other small parasites.

Western chipmunk Length: 18 cm (7 in) Weight: 50 g (1.8 oz)

When eating, a chipmunk uses its front paws like hands.

The chipmunk does not take only dust baths, however. Like a cat, the chipmunk uses its tongue and paws to groom itself. Grooming with the paws also helps to remove extra hairs from the chipmunk's coat. This is especially helpful for chipmunks in northern areas where they shed their coats twice a year.

Getting Around

Chipmunks never seem to walk—they scamper and scurry this way or that at top speed. They are good swimmers and even better climbers. So you need not worry if you see one dangling dangerously from a branch as it reaches for its favorite food. The chipmunk is one of nature's acrobats and it seldom loses its balance. If a chipmunk is being chased, it may even leap from one branch to another in order to escape.

Every autumn, chipmunks exchange their bright summer coat for a less colorful but warmer winter one.

Despite all its fast movements, the chipmunk seldom goes very far from its home. In fact, most chipmunks usually stay within 50 metres (55 yards) or so of their den. This area is called their territory, and they guard it from intruders. If a chipmunk happens to wander into another chipmunk's territory, it will soon find itself chased out. A chipmunk will make exceptions, though, for family members or a would-be mate.

Chipmunk Homes

All chipmunks build underground burrows. Some live in them all year, others for only part of the year.

The pile of soil left behind when the chipmunk builds its burrow could show enemies where to find the opening to its den. Can you guess how the chipmunk solves this problem?

Digging in.

It digs another entrance hole after all the work on the burrow is finished. It then fills the first "work hole" and uses only the new hole to enter and leave its den. For extra safety, the chipmunk hides this entrance to its underground home in a brush heap, under a fallen log or at the base of a tree.

Most burrows have a single tunnel that leads from the entrance to a den that is about the size of a coconut. Here the chipmunk makes a nest of shredded leaves, dried grasses and fluffy seed heads. This will make a soft cushion for new babies or a warm bed in which to spend the winter.

Except for a mother with her babies, chipmunks live alone. Each adult chipmunk has its own den.

Fancy Homes and Plain Ones
The Eastern Chipmunk has only one home. It uses its underground burrow year round and may live in the same one for several years.

But just like people who add new rooms to change their homes, the Eastern Chipmunk will often add new tunnels and rooms. This creates quite a maze of underground passages. The chipmunk may fill in old entrance holes or it may leave them open as emergency escape routes.

Desert-dwelling western chipmunks also live year round in burrows. Other western chipmunks, however, use both an underground den and a high-rise nest in a nearby tree. They use the burrow as a winter home or as a den

The entrance tunnel to a chipmunk's den slopes gradually. The den itself is usually about 30 cm (1 ft) deep.

Eastern Chipmunks often add extra dens and tunnels to their burrow. Notice how the entrances are placed at the base of trees and rocks where they are less likely to be seen.

for the mother and her babies. Unlike the Eastern Chipmunk, they usually build a new burrow each year.

The tree nest is a summer home for adults or for growing youngsters. Made of leaves and grasses, the nest is shaped like a ball and looks like a covered bird's nest. Some chipmunks may even take over a deserted woodpecker's hole for the summer. Chipmunks move into their tree nests when their burrows become too dirty or when their dens become infested with fleas or other parasites.

Most western chipmunks build tree nests which they use in the summer.

Chipmunk Chatter

It is sometimes hard to find even the noisiest chipmunk in the woods because its voice seems to come from different places. But look closely —the chipmunk twitches its tail in time to its call, and this often gives away its hiding spot.

You can often tell what a chipmunk is feeling by listening to the sounds it makes. For instance, it will sometimes show pleasure by making soft noises deep in its throat. And a chipmunk who finds a special treat may chatter with excitement the same way a person might exclaim over a special gift.

A chipmunk has other ways of showing its feelings, too.

Opposite page:
For such a small and charming animal, a chipmunk can look surprisingly fierce when scolding an intruder.

Chipmunks live alone, but if two chipmunks meet they sniff each other's face as a greeting. They are able to recognize brothers and sisters by smell.

21

If the chipmunk sees danger, it will run away quickly with its tail in the air. Sometimes the chipmunk will make a loud chirping call, but often it will be silent, putting all its energy into running.

The chipmunk scolds its enemy or intruders from the safety of a tree. During this loud, noisy chatter, the chipmunk's tail bobs up and down to help him make his point perfectly clear!

When a chipmunk is not sure if danger threatens, it sits up very tensely on its hind legs. It stamps one foot and then the other as it watches.

A Dangerous Life

Like many small animals the chipmunk is important to the balance of nature. It is part of the diet of predators such as coyotes, hawks, weasels, snakes, bobcats and raccoons.

You might think that the tiny chipmunk stands little chance against such animals. But the chipmunk is clever. It hides from predators by staying near plants or fallen logs that give it cover. And if a chipmunk does find itself in danger, it quickly dashes away and climbs the nearest tree or scurries into its underground den.

The chipmunk may avoid most enemies this way, but these tactics do not work so well with the weasel. The weasel is a very fast and very sleek animal. It can catch a running chipmunk and sometimes can even get into its underground burrow. The weasel is also an excellent climber and can follow a chipmunk up into the trees.

The lucky chipmunk that keeps out of the way of its enemies may live for anywhere from three to seven years.

Dinner-time

The types of food that the chipmunk eats will depend on where it lives and the types of food it can find. Generally, it eats mainly plants.

Summer, therefore, is the time when there is plenty to eat. Chipmunks can choose dinner from a variety of fruits and nuts. Their favorite foods include strawberries, blueberries, chokecherries, raspberries, wild grasses and pine seeds.

But some chipmunks live in places where these plants are hard to find. As a result, they must look for other types of food. They may eat wild mushrooms, the roots of certain plants and bird's eggs. Some will even chomp on a grasshopper, beetle or caterpillar. None of us can have our favorite foods all the time and neither can the chipmunk. Any chipmunk will eat many of these other foods when it cannot find seeds and berries.

Some chipmunks even eat flowers!

Whenever possible the chipmunk carries its meal up onto a rock or tree stump, or to some other high spot. There it can keep an eye open for danger while it has dinner.

Unlike you, chipmunks don't need to drink every day. They get most of their water from the plants that they eat. Think of how much water there is in a nice juicy strawberry! Not needing a drink every day is especially important to chipmunks living on the edge of deserts or in other dry areas.

Spring is a tricky time for the chipmunk. The winter store of food has been eaten. New plants are just beginning to grow. At this time, the chipmunk will eat any food it can find— new sprouts, tree buds and any of last year's seeds or nuts that are still lying on the ground.

Perched up on a tree stump a chipmunk can eat and keep watch at the same time.

Gathering and Storing Food

Chipmunks spend most of their day collecting and storing food. They carry away their groceries in their specially built cheek pouches.

These pouches are not wet like the inside of your mouth. They are dry like your skin, so that the food does not get wet when the chipmunk carries it. A chipmunk's cheeks can stretch to carry an amazing number of seeds. One chipmunk was found to be carrying over 3700 blueberry seeds in its cheeks!

In the early summer, chipmunks hide food in many different places. They may simply cover their treasures with fallen leaves or they may dig small holes and bury them. Small seeds are stored in clumps while larger nuts are stored alone.

The chipmunk has keen eyesight and a good nose for finding food. It can easily sniff out

A chipmunk can stuff six chestnuts into its cheeks—three in each side. That may not seem like so very much, but remember: each chestnut is at least as big as the chipmunk's whole HEAD!

buried food stores. But the chipmunk buries so much food that it may forget where some of it is hidden. When this happens the seeds may sprout, growing into plants or even trees. The chipmunk is one of nature's gardeners without even knowing it.

Occasionally other animals, such as squirrels and mice, steal from a chipmunk's food store. But then our friend will also take food from the hiding place of other small animals. So it probably all works out evenly in the end.

Getting Ready for Winter

In late summer, chipmunks in Canada and the northern United States begin to store food in earnest for the long winter. They select seeds and nuts because these will keep well.

To get the seeds from fruits, like choke-cherries, the chipmunk carefully strips off pieces of the flesh with its teeth. It leaves the fruit in a small pile and then carries away the seeds. If you see a mysterious pile of fruit on a fallen log or rock you will know who has been around.

Opposite page:
Whether scamper-ing along the ground or up a tree, a chipmunk pauses every few steps to look and listen for signs of danger.

The chipmunk's special winter store of food is kept under its nest. That way, the chipmunk never has to leave its den for its mid-winter snack. And what a snack! One nest was found with over 68 000 seeds stored under it.

Winter Slumber

Chipmunks need to avoid the harsh winter when it is cold outside and there is not much to eat. They do this by going into hibernation. This means that the chipmunk sleeps through most of the winter. Its body temperature drops and both its breathing and heart beat are much slower. With its body working at such slow speed, the chipmunk does not need much energy to survive the winter.

It does need some, however. Many hibernating animals put on extra fat to help them make it through the winter. The chipmunk does not, and that is why it has to work so hard to store away a good supply of food.

If a chipmunk finds a rich supply of seeds, it will often stuff its cheeks and hide away several loads before it actually eats any.

But, you may wonder, if the chipmunk hibernates, when does it eat? Unfortunately no one knows for sure. Some people think it goes into real hibernation only after it has eaten all of its supply of food. Another possibility is that it wakes up once in a while and eats some of the nuts and seeds it has stored under its nest. Then it goes back to sleep.

In either case, the chipmunk is much warmer snuggled in its cozy nest inside its underground den than it would be outside. A new coat of woolly fur which the chipmunk grows in late summer helps to keep it warm during its sleep.

Chipmunks hibernate for different lengths of time, depending where they live. In Canada, chipmunks usually begin to hibernate in late October or early November and stay in their dens until April. Farther south, the time spent in hibernation is shorter. The milder the winter, the shorter the period of hibernation gets, until it lasts only a few weeks. Where the

winter is very mild, such as in the southern United States, there is no need for chipmunks to hibernate at all. There, you will see them year round.

Striped Sunbathers

On a cold spring or fall day you might see a chipmunk sunbathing. That's right, it will spread itself out on a warm rock and catch some of the sun's warmth. But too much heat makes chipmunks uncomfortable, just as it does you.

So don't expect to see any chipmunks at noon on a really hot day. They will all be keeping cool in their underground burrows. As long as the weather remains very hot, they will come out only during the coolness of the early morning and evening. Chipmunks do not seem to like heavy rain, either. Just as most people do, they scurry for shelter in a storm.

Providing the weather is not too hot, chipmunks like to soak up a bit of sun.

Starting a Family

Mating takes place in early spring. The male chipmunks fight to decide who will father the young. Sometimes one of them will be badly injured by bites. More often, the chipmunk who is losing is smart enough to accept defeat and scamper off before he gets seriously hurt. This fighting is important. It means that only the strongest and healthiest males father the young. This in turn ensures the strongest and healthiest possible offspring. After mating, the male leaves the female and lives alone.

The mother gives birth by herself in her underground den about 30 days after mating. The litter usually consists of four to six tiny babies called pups. The pups are born without hair and are both deaf and blind. They weigh about three grams (one-tenth of an ounce).

Baby chipmunks huddle together in their nest. Their stripes are now quite definite, and they will probably soon be ready to follow their mother on her outings.

Like all mothers, the chipmunk takes good care of her babies, and they nurse many times a day on her rich milk. She will fight any intruder that comes too near her den—including other chipmunks!

Growing Up

After ten days, faint downy hair covers the pups' bodies and the chipmunk stripes begin to show. The babies do not open their eyes or hear properly until the end of their fourth week of life. At this time they are beginning to learn how to walk, stumbling over each other as they move around the den.

Eastern Chipmunk pups remain in their underground burrows, but often western chipmunk babies are moved to a tree nest at their fifth week. The new tree nest is roomier and cleaner than the old burrow, and it may also be safer from enemies.

This could well be this young chipmunk's first look at the outside world.

The mother chipmunk moves the pups one by one to their new home. As she carries them by the skin of their belly, the babies curl in a tight bundle with their head and tail cuddled around her nose.

At six weeks of age the pups are looking more like their parents. Their stripes are quite definite and their tail is getting bushy. The mother is now able to leave them alone for several hours at a time while she searches for food. But she returns often throughout the day to let them nurse.

Soon the young chipmunks are able to leave the nest and explore. They seldom stray very far, however.

On Their Own

About half an hour before sunset, the mother and her young return to the nest area. This is the time to play. The mother chipmunk joins her youngsters in play fights, games of chase and follow the leader. These games are not only fun, they are good training. The young chipmunks become more skilled at climbing

Opposite page:
It is hard to imagine, but just a few weeks ago this proud fellow had a skinny, hairless tail that would look more at home on a rat than on a chipmunk.

and running, and they learn how to escape quickly when being chased.

Bedtime is at sunset. The mother and her babies go into the nest and sleep, cuddled together, until sunrise.

By the time they are ten weeks old, the chipmunks have tried many different foods and they no longer need milk from their mother. They are nearly as big as mom and are ready to leave the nest.

It is late summer by now. Like their parents the young chipmunks must begin to gather food for the winter. They also must build their own winter dens. The next weeks will be very busy for them.

Because they have so much to do before winter, these young chipmunks will be the last to settle down for their long winter sleep.

When they wake up next spring, they will be ready to begin their own families.

High up in the mountains and near the desert's edge, where plants are scarce, chipmunks use boulders and underground tunnels for hiding places.

Special Words

Burrow   A hole in the ground dug by an animal to be used as a home.

Den   Animal home.

Desert   Hot dry area with few plants or trees.

Groom   Brush or clean hair or fur.

Hibernation   Kind of heavy sleep that some animals take in the winter, during which their breathing and heart rates slow, and their body temperatures go down.

Litter   Group of animal brothers and sisters born together.

Mate   To come together to produce young.

Nursing   The drinking of milk from a mother's body.

Parasite   An animal, for example a flea, that lives off of the living bodies of other animals.

Predator   Animal that lives by hunting others for food.

Pup   Baby chipmunk.

Rodent   An animal with a certain kind of teeth, which are especially good for gnawing.

Swamp   Area where the ground is soaked by water.

Territory   Area that an animal or group of animals lives in and often defends from other animals of the same kind.

Work Hole   First tunnel dug by a chipmunk when it is making its burrow.

INDEX

Cover Photo: Bill Ivy.
Photo Credits: Lowry Photo: pages 4, 36; Norman R. Lightfoot; 6, 17, 46; Valan Photos, 9, 27 (Thomas Kitchin), 10 (Esther Schmidt), 14 (Herman H. Giethoorn), 20 (Wayne Lankinen) 24 Albert Kuhnigk, 29 (Harold V. Green), 33 (John Fowler), 35 (Pam Hickman), 42 (J.R. Page); Network Stock Photo File: 30 (Barry Griffiths); Parks Canada: 39 (T. W. Hall); V. Claerhout: 13, 41; Harold R. Hungerford: 45.

Printed and Bound in Spain

Getting To Know...

Nature's Children

BEAVERS

Elin Kelsey

Grolier Limited
TORONTO

PUBLISHER	Joseph R. DeVarennes	
PUBLICATION DIRECTOR	Kenneth H. Pearson	
MANAGING EDITOR	Valerie Wyatt	
SERIES ADVISOR	Merebeth Switzer	
SERIES CONSULTANT	Michael Singleton	
CONSULTANTS	Ross James	
	Kay McKeever	
	Dr. Audrey N. Tomera	
ADVISORS	Roger Aubin	
	Robert Furlonger	
	Gaston Lavoie	
EDITORIAL SUPERVISOR	Jocelyn Smyth	
PRODUCTION MANAGER	Ernest Homewood	
PRODUCTION ASSISTANTS	Penelope Moir	
	Brock Piper	
EDITORS	Katherine Farris	Anne Minguet-Patocka
	Sandra Gulland	Sarah Reid
	Cristel Kleitsch	Cathy Ripley
	Elizabeth MacLeod	Eleanor Tourtel
	Pamela Martin	Karin Velcheff
PHOTO EDITORS	Bill Ivy	
	Don Markle	
DESIGN	Annette Tatchell	
CARTOGRAPHER	Jane Davie	
PUBLICATION ADMINISTRATION	Kathy Kishimoto	
	Monique Lemonnier	
ARTISTS	Marianne Collins	Greg Ruhl
	Pat Ivy	Mary Theberge

This series is approved and recommended by the Federation of Ontario Naturalists.

Canadian Cataloguing in Publication Data

Kelsey, Elin.
  Beavers

(Getting to know—nature's children)
Includes index.
ISBN 0-7172-1894-5

1. Beavers—Juvenile literature. I. Title
II. Series.

QL737.R632K45 1984   j599.32′32   C84-099386-2

Have you ever wondered . . .

When you think of beavers, the first thing that probably comes to mind is the expression "busy as a beaver." People have been thinking of beavers as eager, hard workers for a long time. For example, there is an Indian legend that tells of the Great Spirit building the earth with the help of beavers. This would certainly have been a big enough job to keep a lot of beavers very busy. And it would have been a good job for them because they are excellent builders.

Now let's find out what makes beavers such good builders and what is keeping them so busy today.

Beavers: Who and Where

There are some beavers in Europe and Asia, but most of them live in Canada and the United States.

The beaver has no close relatives, but it does have some distant cousins. You can recognize them by their teeth. All beavers have big, very sharp front teeth that they use for cutting. Squirrels, rats, and gophers have sharp front cutting teeth too. Scientists call animals that have special teeth like these rodents. The name comes from a word that means "to gnaw or chew"—which is just what all rodents love to do!

Where beavers are found in North America.

Beavers Up Close

The sturdy beaver is the largest rodent in North America. You would have to be quite strong to lift an adult beaver. In fact, if an average-sized eight-year-old and a beaver were sitting on either end of a teeter-totter, their weights would about balance.

An Amazing Tail

There is no mistaking a beaver's wide, scaly tail. It looks like a pine cone that has been flattened by a steam-roller! This amazing tail serves many purposes. When the beaver is swimming, it steers itself through the water by shifting its tail from side to side. If it is towing a heavy log, it moves its tail to balance the weight. A frightened beaver slaps its tail against the water with a loud *thwack*! The sound tells other beavers to dive for safety.

A Beautiful Coat

The beaver's coat may not be as remarkable as its tail, but it is much more beautiful. It is soft and silky, and can range from golden brown

to rich, dark brown in color. It is also very warm—which is probably more important from the beaver's point of view!

Why is the beaver's coat so warm? Because it has two layers. The outer layer is made up of long shiny "guard" hairs. Underneath, is a thick, woolly layer of shorter fur. It is a coat worth taking good care of, and beavers do just that. They even have a built-in comb for the purpose—two double claws on each hind foot. These claws can open and close, rather like a pair of tiny pliers, and the beaver uses them to untangle its fur and to comb out any twigs or clumps of dirt.

As well, all beaver have a pair of glands near their tails where a special oil is made. They spread this oil through their fur with their paws. Even after an hour of swimming, a beaver's body stays dry and cozy inside its oily, waterproofed coat.

Beaver paw prints.

In the wintertime keeping warm and dry is especially important to the beaver. This beaver is grooming its fur to get ready for the swim home.

This waterproofing is important because beavers spend much of their time cutting and peeling branches underwater. Most animals would soon get waterlogged if they tried this, but beavers never do. They have furry lips that close behind their front teeth to keep the water out, so they can work just as well underwater as they can on land.

Very near the glands where oil is made is another set of glands, called castors, where castoreum is made. Castoreum is a strong-smelling oily substance with which beavers mark their ponds and lodges to let other beavers know who lives there.

Seeing, Smelling and Hearing

Beavers have very small ears and eyes. But their hearing is excellent, and they see quite well—at least in daylight. They find seeing in the dark just as hard as you do, however. Yet beavers do most of their work at night. Instead of relying on their eyesight, they use their sharp senses of smell and hearing to direct them and alert them to danger.

Front paw.

Back paw.

Champions in the Water

With a flat tail for steering and strong, webbed back feet to supply the power, beavers are perfect water travellers. Their bodies are streamlined for swimming. Holding its tiny fists tight against its chest, a beaver glides through the water with only its head above the surface.

Beavers are also terrific underwater swimmers. Their large lungs can store lots of air, and most beavers can hold their breath for about ten minutes.

No matter what kind of fancy flips and dives a beaver makes, it is never bothered by water getting into its nose or ears. Beavers have special muscles that seal their nostrils and ears when they are diving.

A beaver's eyes are protected too. Thanks to an extra pair of see-through eyelids that close over its eyes, a beaver can see just as well underwater as it can above.

Clumsy on Land

Getting around on land is another story. Imagine playing tag in the woods with swim fins on your feet. You would trip all over your big, floppy feet and be easy to catch. Beavers have the same problem. With webbed back feet the size of ping-pong paddles, beavers are very slow and awkward on land.

For beavers, water means safety. When they do have to go ashore to cut trees, they listen and sniff the air carefully to make sure no one is coming.

The more a beaver uses its teeth, the sharper they become.

Special Teeth for Special Food

A beaver's front teeth are very special. Like your fingernails, these large teeth never stop growing. A beaver must chew to trim its teeth just as you must clip your nails to keep them from getting too long.

The outer surface of these front teeth has an incredibly strong orange coating. As the beaver chews through pieces of wood, the backs of the teeth wear down faster than the strong orange fronts. The more a beaver uses its teeth, the sharper they get for cutting.

The beaver's back molars are special too. They are as sharp and bumpy as a cheese grater. A beaver uses these teeth to grind up about 500 grams (more than a pound) of tree bark every day.

Special Food

You may prefer ice cream, but tree bark is a beaver's favorite food. When a beaver is eating, it looks just like someone enjoying a cob of corn. It holds and turns a branch between its paws as it nibbles away at the tasty bark. Beavers do most of their feeding inside their homes or in the water where they are safest from hungry animals.

One good thing about eating tree bark is that you can always have a snack before the hard work of cutting down a tree.

In the spring and summer, beavers like to eat juicy shrubs and tree buds. During the fall, they eat more bark than usual and put on extra fat for the winter. They cut down many trees and gnaw them into short pieces. These are stored in big underwater piles near their homes. When the ice freezes over the top of their pond, the beavers have enough food stored to last the winter.

It doesn't happen often, but some winters the pond may freeze all the way through. Unable to swim to their underwater food store, the beavers could die of hunger. But beavers are lucky. Their homes are built from the same thing they eat—branches! As long as the winter doesn't last too long, the beavers can survive by eating bits of their home.

A tender summer leaf is always good for a nibble.

The Beaver At Work

If you have ever had the painful experience of biting your tongue, you know how strong your chewing muscles are. A beaver's chewing muscles are much stronger than yours. With these powerful muscles and its very sharp teeth, a single beaver may cut down more than 200 trees every year!

When cutting, a beaver stands on its hind legs and leans back against its broad tail. It cuts with its head held sideways. The grooves left by the beaver's sharp teeth run across the tree trunk in the same direction as the marks left by an axe.

Beavers are messy workers. Instead of chewing out neat slices, a beaver takes several bites from the top of a cut and several bites from the bottom. Then it yanks out the wood that is left in the middle. The beaver's top teeth do most of the cutting while the bottom teeth help to steady its mouth.

Grooves left by beaver's teeth.

22

Many people think that a beaver can make a tree fall whichever way it wants. It cannot, and it does not even know which way a tree it is cutting will fall. That is why a beaver cuts only until its teeth feel the last bits of wood just starting to break. Then—*swoosh!*—the beaver dashes for the safety of its pond.

The crash of the falling tree can be heard all over the forest. Before leaving the pond, the beaver waits and sniffs the air to make sure that no hungry bears or cougars have followed the sound in search of a beaver lunch.

Getting it Home
When all seems safe, the beaver and its family will begin cutting off the branches and dragging them back to their pond. If a log is too heavy for one beaver to carry in its mouth, two beavers will work together, rolling the log along the ground with their front paws.

It can seem like a long way to the pond when you have to drag a branch this size with you.

24

Once the trees near the pond are used up, beavers may have to move the logs quite a distance. Sometimes, when this happens, they dig canals that carry water from the pond closer to the trees. Then they can simply float the heavy logs back home. Beavers have been known to dig canals as much as 100 metres (328 feet) long.

Building the Dam

The perfect beaver pond is deep and surrounded by lots of trees. Beavers need to build their homes in deep ponds so that the underwater entrances are well covered. They also need deep water to keep the pond from freezing solid in the winter. To make their ponds deep enough, beavers build dams.

A dam works like the plug in your bathtub. The plug stops the tap water from running down the drain. Beavers build dams across the low banks or creeks where water could flow out of their ponds. With these exits sealed, the water from incoming streams gets trapped in the pond, making it very deep.

Nature's Engineers

Beavers are born knowing how to build dams. They start their building by holding large sticks in their mouths and driving them straight into the river bottom. Almost everything that a beaver can find goes into the dam—wood, grass, rocks and sometimes an old flashlight or shoe.

A beaver dam is built like a layer cake. Just as the cake is held together by layers of icing, the dam is held together by layers of mud. It is sometimes said that beavers use their tails to hammer in branches and spread mud when building dams, but this is not true. Beavers use

To keep the water where they want it, beavers must always be ready to patch up their dams.

their paws and noses to smear the mud over their dam.

Beavers will build until the sound of water running out of their pond has stopped. This sound is such an important signal for the beavers that scientists have been able to trick them into building dams by playing tape recordings of trickling water sounds.

Beaver Meadows

People get angry when a beaver's dam floods a road or field. It is true that beaver dams can sometimes be a nuisance, but they can be useful too—and not just to beavers! Beaver ponds become home to many new plants and animals. Grazing cattle often drink from them. And many years later, after the dam has rotted away and the pond has dried up, the soil will be very rich for farming. This land, which was once covered by a beaver pond, is known as a beaver meadow.

A Home of Sticks and Mud

When the dam is finished, the beavers start to work on a home. There is a lot of variety in beaver homes—in fact, no two are exactly alike.

If the beavers live in a pond that has very high banks they may simply dig a burrow in the side and live there. When the banks are low, beavers build a special kind of home—called a lodge—in their pond.

Building the Lodge

The beavers start their lodge by anchoring sticks in the bottom of the pond and piling a huge mound of branches on top. With every member of the family helping, the mound soon reaches high above the water. The branches are cemented together with thin mud. Carrying the mud in their paws or under their chins, the beavers dash as far up the slippery sides of the lodge as they can get. The mud that they dump flows down the sides, covering the lodge like syrup on a stack of pancakes.

Because the beavers seldom make it all the way up, the top gets very little mud. The mudless roof is important. It allows plenty of fresh air to get in the lodge.

Making it Comfortable
When the outside is almost finished, the beavers dive under water and begin to chew a tunnel through to the centre of the mound. They make a large living room above water level and then cut out at least one more entrance tunnel. The doorways to the tunnels are hidden underwater so that bears and wolves will not be able to get in.

Beavers will stay in the same pond and live in the same lodge as long as there are plenty of trees in the area. Like most homeowners, they spend a lot of time improving their lodges. As the family grows, additions are built to make the lodge roomy enough for everyone.

When there is work to be done, the whole beaver colony pitches in.

This is what you might see if you could slice off one side of a typical beaver lodge. While from the outside the lodge looks like a pile of sticks, inside it is a comfortable home.

During the winter, the beaver family stays warm by snuggling together inside their home. Even when the temperature outside drops to -50°C, (-58°F) the heat of the beavers' bodies keeps the inside of the lodge above the freezing point. A blanket of snow on the lodge helps trap heat inside too.

When a beaver gets hungry in the winter, it takes a deep breath and swims out the tunnel to the underwater food pile that was built in the fall.

The Beaver Family

Cows live in herds and chickens live in flocks. But beavers live in family groups just as you do. A beaver family is called a colony.

A mother and father beaver stay together for their whole lives. Though both parents help to raise the babies, it is the mother who makes the final decisions in a beaver colony.

Beavers mate each year in late January or early February. During the breeding season, the beaver pair spend a lot of time frolicking and play-wrestling below the icy covering of their pond. The beavers mate during some of these underwater play sessions.

A female beaver has to wait three and a half months for her babies to be born. While she is waiting, she prepares a special nursery inside the lodge. She builds warm, comfortable beds for her babies by splitting soft wood into thin chips.

A beaver mother likes to be alone when her babies are born. Shortly before they arrive, the father leaves the lodge and moves into a burrow on the edge of the pond. When the birth time comes, the mother beaver sits up with her tail between her legs and carefully licks each baby as it is born. Beavers usually have a litter of four babies, called kits.

Beaver kits are born with a tiny set of sharp front teeth, a thick furry coat, and a flat scaly tail.

Beaver Babies

Weighing a little more than a baseball, each wide-eyed kit looks like a tiny copy of its parents. It even has a tiny set of sharp front teeth.

Beaver kits never need to take swimming lessons. They can swim a few hours after they are born! Their thick fur coats trap so much air that the kits bob along the water surface like corks. In fact, the babies float so well that they cannot dive until they have gained a few pounds. But since a floating kit would be an easy catch for a hungry hawk or otter, the mother keeps her babies inside the lodge for the first two months.

Just like new human babies, beaver kits wake up every few hours and cry to be fed. They often sit on their mother's tail when they are nursing. Beaver milk is butter-yellow and as thick as toothpaste. This rich milk helps the babies grow quickly.

Beaver parents teach their kits to dive when they hear a tail slap against the water.

A Lot to Learn

The kits learn many things by copying their parents and older brothers and sisters. When they see an older beaver chewing on a leaf, they rush over to have a taste. If another beaver dives for a branch, they dive too.

One important lesson the kits must learn is how to recognize danger. They are taught to sniff the air for the smell of wolves, cougars and bears and to watch and listen for otters, hawks and owls.

Both beaver parents are quick to help a whining kit. They will often carry them from danger by holding them in their mouths or scooping them up in their arms.

Growing Up

Beaver youngsters live with their parents for two years. Since a new litter is born every year, this means that a typical beaver family has about ten members—mother and father, one-year-olds (called yearlings) and kits.

The yearlings usually move out with their father for two weeks or so when the new litter

is being born. By this time, they are helping with the cutting and carrying chores, and with any needed repairs to the dam or lodge.

At two years of age, the young beavers are ready to leave home. They have to leave to make room for a new litter of kits. Most of them go quite willingly, but once in a while a straggler needs to be sent off with a hiss or a slap.

The young beavers may travel far before they settle down. Most, however, will pick a spot within 10 kilometres (6 miles) of their parents' pond. They soon find mates and set to work busily building dams and lodges for their own new colonies.

Special Words

Breeding season   The time of year during which animals will mate.

Burrow   A hole in the ground dug by an animal to be used as a home.

Canal   A path that is dug out for water to follow.

Castoreum   Special substance produced by the beaver's body and used to mark its territory.

Colony   A family of beavers living together.

Dam   A kind of wall built to hold back water.

Guard hairs   Long coarse hairs that make up the outer layer of the beaver's coat.

Kit   Name for the young of various animals including the beaver.

Litter   Group of animal brothers and sisters born together.

Lodge   Beaver home built in the water, out of logs, sticks and mud.

Mate   To come together to produce young.

Molars   Large back teeth used for grinding.

Nursing   The drinking of milk from a mother's body.

Rodent   An animal with a certain kind of teeth, which are especially good for gnawing.

Territory   Area that an animal or group of animals lives in and often defends from other animals of the same kind.

Webbed feet   Feet like those of the beaver and the duck, for example, in which the toes are joined together by flaps of skin.

Yearling   Animal that is one year old.

INDEX

Cover Photo: Valan Photos, Wayne Lankinen
Photo Credits: Network Stock Photo File: page 4 (Jacob Formsma); Valan Photos:
6, 42 (J.A. Wilkinson), 9, 45 (Wayne Lankinen), 13 (John Fowler), 16 (Harold
V. Green), 19, 29 (Dennis W. Schmidt), 25 (Val & Alan Wilkinson), 26 (Brian
Milne); Norman R. Lightfoot: 10, 15, 30, 33, 39, 41; Lowry Photography: 20,
23; NFB Phototèque: 34:

Printed and Bound in Spain